AMPERSAND

Lydia Fulleylove is a freelance writer and teacher who lives on the Isle of Wight. She has worked extensively in prisons, healthcare and with young people and leads community cross arts projects, often inspired by sea and landscape. She loves sea swimming and walking in wild places. Her first collection, *Notes on Sea and Land* was published by Happen*Stance* Press and her second collection *Estuary*, with artist Colin Riches, was published by Two Ravens Press.

—

Evelyn Wilkinson (1920 – 2007) was born in Lancashire. She joined the Women's Auxiliary Air Force in 1942 and became a radar operator. During the 1960s she became a lecturer in Drama at La Sainte Union College of Education in Southampton where she worked until her retirement in 1983. In 1984 she published *Starting Points in Drama* (Kemble Press), a handbook for teachers. Drawing and painting remained integral parts of her life and her sketchbook was always at hand to the very end.

Ampersand

LYDIA FULLEYLOVE

& Evelyn M. Wilkinson

Valley Press

First published in 2022 by Valley Press
Woodend, The Crescent, Scarborough, YO11 2PW
www.valleypressuk.com

ISBN 978-1-912436-89-7
Cat. no. VP0203

Cover and text design by Peter Barnfather.
Edited by Jo Brandon.

Printed and bound in Great Britain by
Imprint Digital, Upton Pyne, Exeter.

Contents

Introduction

After my mother died in 2007, I discovered in a cupboard – under the eaves – the diaries which she had written while in the Women's Auxiliary Air-force (The WAAF), from 1942 to 1945. We had spoken once or twice of reading them together, but we had never done so. Perhaps we didn't need to, because when I began to read them her young voice spoke to me as clearly as if she had been there beside me. The rhythms of her prose worked their way into my consciousness and I'd find myself saying lines aloud when immersed in something else.

Throughout her life, she often spoke to me of her belief in using all experiences creatively, both in relation to her work as a visual artist and drama teacher, and to mine as a teacher and a writer. In her war diaries she wrote about this need to transform experience *however bewildering or heart-rending. Can I make something of it with paint and line or will it be a group of rhythmic phrases or regular cadences?*

What could I make from her diaries? My first attempt was to re-draft her entries as poems, using small shifts, line breaks and edits to create a series of couplets and quatrains. Later, in discussion with a fellow writer, I realised that this compromised the integrity of the original – of her own words as she had thought and shaped them from day to day, in her often lyrical prose.

What if I, instead, wrote a series of poems in response to selected diary extracts? What if the text became a dialogue between our two voices, a kind of collaboration between past and present, between my mother and myself, revealing our posthumous relationship through re-awakened memories and fresh awareness of our sometimes mirrored lives?

So, here am I, past middle age, in conversation with my mother aged twenty-two.

Before I read
my mother's diaries

what I need to say to myself is this:
don't squander this one chance

of reaching them fresh, unread
by anyone but her. Hold back

till you're ready to touch her words,
to empty your head.

Here they are. Feel their spines.
Worn smooth. The rub of years.

The blue one, the red one, the green,
the one with the flush of flowers.

Finger a page. The rush of vowels.
Familiar flourish of an *F* or a *J*.

Fifteenth January 1942, Gloucester

It is cold; there are fluctuating waves of femininity in a bewildering chaos of colour, punctuated with the official blue uniforms. I am in the W.A.A.F. An appalling journey, a long wait on Gloucester platform with fifty or so of my kind, & a bewildering & shaking ride in a bus that appeared to be a near relation to a Black Mariah. The next few hours, a nightmare of official forms, labyrinthine alleys between huts, dustbins & cabbage patches. A cold supper in a bare & vast dining room is not very cheering, nor is a hair, chest & hands examination on top of a long journey. However, bed at last, cold, hard & very flat, in the company of 28 others, only to rise at six & polish the hut floor.

Ampersand

Like you, the Romans used a cursive script which meant
that when they wrote *et*, the word for *and*,

they joined the *e* and *t* and this became the ampersand
which skipped across the centuries,

loped along your lines. It's hard to let it go, although
once translated to whichever laptop font

it loses flair. I discover that in film credits
the use of *&*, the logogram, denotes a closer collaboration

between artists than the use of *and*
and I wonder if, out of your words and mine,

something – someone – new, is in the making.

Twenty-first March 1942, Morecambe

If Gloucester was cold & frozen, Morecambe is bitter & windy. The wind whistles round those terraces of tall black boarding houses. We seem to be always wearing our groundsheets, & the wind tugs them out into wild, billowing shapes, until our own figures, marching up & down the promenade, become grotesque & swollen. The town seethed with girls in Air Force blue, & to their landladies they were more unpopular than the RAF who had been there before. This was probably due to the fact that women are more exacting than men, demanding above all plenty of hot water. Many landladies limited our washing to stockings and handkerchiefs only and this led to a great deal of furtive washing in the billets & resultant sanctions. Around all this there were constant lectures on service procedure, daily drill and inspections and the ever present excitement over expected postings. At last we were posted on our various courses & I came with Norah to Bridgenorth on the Admin' course. Few of us enjoyed the 14 day training. The drill 'got us down' more than anything else, & our dark forms are to be seen on the parade ground after dark, feverishly drilling one another …

'Square-bashing'

printed in turquoise ink
on the back of a sepia snapshot

two rows of WAAFS
alert   upright

buttoned tight
into great-coats

hands gloved   crossed in laps
caps set straight

twenty pairs of laced-up feet
aligned   neat

– though now I notice yours
planted childlike   wider apart

and your eyes   not front
as if you weren't

as I'd thought
always pirouetting in the light

but bashful like me
gazing   slant

… then, unfortunately, I had to go into Cosford RAF Hospital for more operations & experiments upon my leg. I was glad of that experience, & I spent nine weeks there before going to East Grinstead Hospital in June 1942 …

Third September 1942, Cosford RAF Hospital

Three years at war. I remember that first Sunday when war came.

Twenty-third March 2020, Isle of Wight

Three weeks of Covid. I remember that last day of our holiday on La Palma.

I was looking after evacuees brought from London to Yarmouth by boat.

We'd seen photos of health-workers in protective suits, goggles, white masks. We'd just heard a case had been reported on Tenerife. That close. Even then, it felt unreal

Crowds of them on the sands, and sleeping on sacks in the Floral Hall.

but we washed our hands with extra care as we waited for the plane. *Does it matter if the water is hot or cold?* someone asked.

Masses of tired children, nursing mothers with small live bundles, that had to be washed & fed under the most trying conditions.

On the train from Gatwick we felt unease as a boy, face withdrawn into his hoodie, coughed harshly.

Then that queer, excitedly expectant solemnity at the announcement of war over the wireless.

Then, tonight, that sudden – solemnity – as the Prime Minister spoke to the nation.

There was relief also, in spite of the pangs of anxiety, a bold rushing chivalrous relief…

There was relief also, in spite of apprehension, that restrictions were being enforced. A breath released.

Fifteenth September 1942, Cosford Hospital

The day of my 8th operation. As yet I have not felt any of the usual paralysing suspense of waiting, perhaps because I'm not really thinking about it.

Twenty-fifth March 2020, Isle of Wight

The second day of lockdown. We are waiting for Covid 19 to peak, in about three weeks. Though I know that more people die each day, I haven't yet felt its impact and often I'm not really thinking about it.

I am thinking of the summer that is slowly dying, & whose frail warmth may at any time be flung with a hail of shrivelled leaves & pinched & lifeless forms at my sad feet.

I'm thinking of the spring. I walk through a tunnel of blackthorn blossom onto Northcourt Down, trying not to crush violets underfoot as I cross the chalk slopes.

I have loved this last part of the summer

I love this time of year – and the new quietness of sky and land,

& the times we spent lying in the clover field under the sun.

the days when we eat lunch outside in the sheltered spot by the kitchen window,

We – James, Ethel, Sergeant Palmer and myself.

Richard and myself on the bench and Polly, our ginger cat, curled among forget-me-nots, celandine and catmint.

Tall, feathery waving grass, purple clover, softly vivid blue sky, dark & dustily green trees.

Fennel feathering the wall, red dead-nettle rampaging, a hazy blue sky and our bodies absorbing a moment of sunshine and ease.

And four healthy young bodies, all shouting defiance at the coldness & death of the coming winter.

Human beings may be dying of the virus all over the world, but perhaps the wild will sprawl into the pauses, the spaces we leave.

Thirtieth June 1942, Cosford Hospital

I enjoyed yesterday to the utmost of my capacity. I have always wondered just what the atmosphere of a theatre is like with an operation in progress. Physically it is hot; psychically not as strained or as frigidly tense as I had expected.

On the couch

We used to curl up with you on the couch,
a nap after lunch, my sister in front,

me tucked behind the crook of your knee.
Even then we knew not to touch your 'bad leg'.

The scar spread more than the breadth of a man's span
from the edge of your knee-bone, reaching across your
shin,

the skin, a thin shiny gauze
through which you'd peer back through the years

to East Grinstead '42. Here with plastic skill
McIndoe re-built burnt faces, cut from your legs

strange knots of nevus veins. Months of operations,
grafts, salt baths but compensations too, as when

they let you *sketch the whole of one op –*
the man with the hare lip,

or when you realized
that mind and spirit burn

through a morass of deformities
and couldn't grumble about your own wounds.

Thirty-first October 1942, Bedford

I have been home nearly a fortnight & so we have another week
of my sick leave left. To be home, to see again the friendly rows
of books striping the dark shelves. I can take down whichever
book I feel like, I can potter around with my paints & brushes,
or I can take my bike, & ride out into the Autumn. In fact,
for the space of 21 days, I am MYSELF.

I take your line

and ride out across the page
this grey November morning.

Pedalling is what I do, have done for years,
the switchback island roads, fog, ice

that slick wet afternoon of tarmac crash,
pain screaming down the nerves –

but the bike's still part of me, transport yes,
but more than that, a steadying

or sometimes an opening up
or letting something go.

My old white bike – drop handlebars,
far outdated derailleur gears –

I leave her unlocked on cliffs,
propped against hedges,

flat on her side when there's nowhere to lean,
unsteal-able, rust-streaked, swift.

Eighth November 1942, Bedford (on leave)

Why do I like Bedford so much? Any casual visitor would think
of it as an ordinary, provincial town, within easy reach of London.
They might find the flatness trying, the streets in the centre of
the town narrow… But that is not the real Bedford. I think the
fact the place is filled with schools, churches & second hand
bookshops has something to do with it… Then there are the
books peeping out of the windows of private houses. Books

sprouting up at the bottom of a bedroom window, clasped together by book ends; book laden shelves, lit up by the firelight of a downstairs room… And the river, insinuating itself under the bridges… Queer how one can grow to love a town. But there it is, & once a place has hold of you, you can never shake it off.

Once a place has hold of you – you can never shake it off

why do I like Bedford so much?
the flatness trying   the streets too narrow
or I this Island? tidy? crowded? tame?
a frame too tight will hem you in   you said to me

by then I'd glimpsed its streaks of wild
frayed cliff tops   collide of currents   curl of surf
sleek sandstone rocks with ripple-marks and rain-prints
where if I face south west
horizon is the only boundary
the far-out boom   the mid-sea rush   the close-up hiss of waves
no human sounds   no land until Brazil
no footprints but mine

close to the end
as if something were suddenly clear
you looked across from Lepe and said

there's Lydia's Island
                        that's Lydia's place

contrary   I said   *it's time to leave*   you said   *don't go*

so we were fixed   closely aligned
opposites   till after your death

now   however hard I strain
to break its hold on me
I still can't shake it off

... the feel of books, the stiffness of clothbound covers, that
crackling, try to resist the attempt of any new buyer to open
them. The lovely rich suppleness of leather bound books with
their silky gilt edges, & the sumptuous gold lettering of their
titles. And the musty, browsy & wistfully reminiscent smell of the
old second hand bookshop, with its rows of dusty, sad looking
castaways, yearning to be once again in the hand of some friendly
& discriminating reader.

Years later –

you tell me how you held
the whole of Shakespeare, not the text

recalled from that first read, but the books
themselves – two volumes bound in leather

with yellowed pages – propped, unwieldy.
My father remembers plain *Warwick*,

neat editions, slipped into a boy's pocket.
I pick *Villette*, the turquoise-black of glittering

paper-back, clasped as I ran to school;
William, scraped knees, skewed grin,

the scrimshank lad clambering the print;
Jane Eyre, dark green, the spine broken,

the pages, thin as sloughed skin,
the whiff of autumn, thickened air.

Twenty-first December 1942, Yatesbury Radar Defence School

I should have liked to have stayed at Gloucester over Christmas but other powers decided differently. So here I am, surrounded by an entirely new group of girls, on my Radar Defence Operations course... Life seems so odd without Nancy. We only knew each other just over five weeks, & yet the first day we met, we knew one another. There was no tentative groping or feeling towards each other, it was as though the hands of our souls had grasped from the first. This seldom happens with me, but when it does, it seems so natural, that I hardly notice it until it's happened. This is one of the worst aspects of the Services, the constant losing of one's friends. Of course there are always others to meet, but the human heart – for all that has been said about its fickleness – demands steadfastness.

Questions to ask the dead or gone

Is memory steadfast?

Why did you keep her photo all these years,
not in an album, but intimate,
tucked away in a thin pink envelope,
held in a yellowed three-inch cardboard frame,
the black curls, the smiling gaze barely faded –
from Nancy inscribed in a strong hand?
Five weeks you knew her.
But did she live on in you until your death,
her shadowy presence flickering
through your diary lines?

And why have I kept this photo of one I loved
stowed in the sleeve of my old *Filofax*?
She's sprawled in her mango fleece in the tent we shared,
The Irish Times spread on the groundsheet,
a small bottle of whisky tilted against the drizzle,
her green bike and mine leant on a rock.
Five years I knew her.
She's not dead but cut off –
a time-flap shut. So why is her absence
still a faint presence inside me?

Or is absence the same as death?
Are you, my mother, a present absence or an absent presence?
Perhaps I need to let you flow until you stop –
like words eventually petering out?
Since the pair of you have – *vanished* – let's try that –
I live – sometimes content –
your absence now as familiar
as your presence –
perhaps that's all we need
to go on

Twenty-seventh December 1942, Yatesbury

And so Christmas has slipped away…

On Christmas morning we had fresh eggs for breakfast, so we all got up. The state of the hut that morning! Holly & yew spread themselves over the walls, Christmas cards flaunted their brave greetings from the tops of crude tin lockers, beds were unstacked, gloriously disarrayed with paper, string & rumpled clothes.

Each Christmas you cleaned the silver
clicking open the old leather cases,

buffing heavy knives, forks
a pair of candlesticks…

The Christmas fever of excitement reached its pitch about dinner time at 12.40. But half an hour before, the queue stretched nearly half way across the parade ground. When at last we were let in, there were hardly enough seats for everyone. For the first time since I've been in the services I saw cloths on the tables, (really sheets) & down the centres of the tables, arranged alternately were mince pies & apples. And then, the noise & eating began. First came platefuls of roast turkey, pork, roast potatoes, sausage, stuffing, sprouts & apple sauce, gingerly carried, four plates at a time, by the officers. Down the long tables they were passed, amid much jocularity, conjured to fit the season.

The thin silver sixpence
slipped into the pudding

the china angel
with tattered tinselled wings

Bottles of beer & lemonade made an uproarious appearance. Corks flew & abnormal stretches of the imagination were created into cocktails. Clamping together & sounding off the whole came waves of singing – slightly raucous but merry, regiments of speeches marched out, & surrounding all with its aroma of correct Christmas sentimentality, hung boughs of mistletoe, shedding its cold yellow-green mystery over the proceedings below.

You made us pale green party frocks –
puffed silk sleeves and sashes.

Later, you gave us tights, soap, swimming goggles –
always a book about cats

and once, towards the end,
although your eyes were dimming,

a camisole, on which you embroidered
with patient love I barely recognised –

pink star-flowers.

Towards evening hilarity once more bounded over, & leaped towards the NAAFI huts, where the dances were being held. All available WAAF were literally grabbed & carried towards the dances. As 12 o'clock drew near, the merriment gradually slipped out into the cold night, & made its way to blankets & bed. Dust subsided, laughter faded up into that clear star eyed Christmas night. Washed yellow by the moon, the parade ground was a wide clean beach, from which the sea has just crept …

When did you stop going up to the loft
to unpack the old wooden stable –

small enough to fit on the side-table –
where you unwrapped

tiny china figures, oxen, sheep?

Seventeenth January 1943, Radar Defence Training Camp, Yatesbury

We are living in a very bleak and lonely spot of the Wiltshire Downs, which in rainy weather is anything but desirable. But today, when everything is gold and blue – like a creation by Van Gogh – nothing could be lovelier. Flat supple rolls of hills, bare except for occasional knots of trees; & here & there, like small grass green bubbles, old barrows covering the regal dust of ancient kings. It is very lovely, but people still refuse to see it, & grumble at the grey white mud to which the camp is attached. But lord! How the grey white mud of the camp blinds our eyes & prevents us from seeing.

Limerstone Down

across the marsh
towards the down
the crack and snap
of frozen grass
the slant path up

the blackthorn coombe
in lichen-light
a kestrel starts
a raven *krarks*
scrub lit by frost
the dance of feet
on chalk, mud, flint
I look up – out
from self – from thought

Tenth February 1943, Downderry

I don't think anyone can fail to remember the sudden quickening of excitement on first sighting the sea after months of inland living …

Coming to Downderry

St Pancras, Paddington,
down to Ashburton –

lured by the lilt
of your prose –

the signing of chits
the slinging of kit

the back of the lorry,
Totness, St Germans

wind strong from the Channel
first sight of blue water

sprayed over the reefs
& the rocks of red cliffs

squeezed between kitbags
we lean out the back

& draw deep breaths
of salty air –

or should I meet you
with my own diary's lines –

the heave-ho greeting of the sea
a map of wave-lap-light

from tousle-headed rocks
sea calls me in –

somehow a village by the sea
never leaves you feeling lonely –

– somehow I walk out of myself
and into the sea –

even if I were never
to make any friends

there would always be
the grey, green, blue & silver sea

sea-shriven – no voice within
only sea-wind on skin

it is the sea you see we say
        it is the sea

Tenth February 1943, Downderry

… there would always be the pools in the rocks, lined with pink
seaweed …

    years later I went to Downderry
    coast road uncoiling

    bleak granite hamlets
    red rocks   seaspray

    tide baring pools
    lined with pink seaweed

    sough of sea-wind
    dream steamer wailing

    nothing in focus till now
    like ink un-fading

    like seeing it
    through the lens of your eye

Twenty-eighth February 1943, Downderry

So this is today & what should have been happy & elated because of a free day, is depressed & disgruntled – & all because of
a stupid row in the hut. But yesterday was lovely. I went to see
the Anglo-Polish ballet in the afternoon. Instead of disharmony,

arguments & irritating regularity, all was colour & rhythm, the meaning of music & form, loveliness & constant change. For two hours, we lived in another world. We lost our awkward limbs & modern clothes & became one with those dancing, weaving bodies.

our words dance

So this was one Good Friday which we shared, twenty years ago. What should have been a day of stillness fractured, all because of a stupid row over lunch: spiked comments, hurt silences, taut necks, wrong notes. But later, someone – was it you? – switched Miles Davis on.

the rhythm shifts

So what? So what?

first you, then me, we're up

our tethered feet feel out the beat

our shoulders ease, our stiff limbs weave

all griefs   for now   released

Eleventh March 1943, Downderry

And the days hurry by with similarity & difference, so that a new week begins before the old one has realized itself… These evenings round the stove in the hut. Wendy brought back a dozen eggs, & we boil them in a saucepan bought in Looe, & then use the water to fill our hot water bottles. We make cocoa & toast bread, sit on the beds, drawn round the stove, & mend or read, & everything is sounded by small chatter & sudden bursts of laughter.

Mending

Hard to imagine
mending stockings

when holey tights
go in the bin,

but from your old workbox I unearth
cotton spools, lozenge tins –

poppers, pins, scraps of chalk
and *Trixie Mercurised Mending* –

flesh-pink, fine spun
specially suitable for

Lisle silk & art silk hose
finer than the thread drawn

by girls' quick fingers
out-in – out-in

as water bubbled in the pan
and you gossiped round the stove

and here – scratched, cross-hatched, worn –
is your old darning needle.

Sometimes, I glimpse you darning
giving my dad's old socks their last innings –

to darn, the verb itself
worn thin

as your skin.

Twenty-seventh March 1943, Downderry

I have not yet recorded our watch party which took place a week
ago. There were seven of us, two men & five girls. We left the
camp by the 11 o'clock Plymouth bus, on a fine spring morning
when sea & red earth were covered with the faint blue haze of
the coming year... We wandered through those grey, shattered
ruins, row after row, dead and silent. The very pavements pathet-
ically waiting for familiar footsteps, while the lamp posts stand
by writhing in iron agony. In the centre of the town, among
the big blocks of stubble and twisted girders, once the stores, are
erected small wooden notices, like crosses to dead soldiers,
proclaiming the name and business of the vanished firm.

It should have been depressing, this nakedness of war, but perhaps through constant nearness, we have become inoculated against it, & so passed through that day in spring with laughter on our lips, & eyes that saw beyond the death lurking beneath those sad grey stones. We followed Drake onto the Hoe in the early afternoon, walked over the springy turf & looked down onto the sparkling Sound with its huddle of ships & aircraft. Tea was late but we had it in the famous Imperial restaurant where we were fed by a Greek waitress on Greek omelette & Apple Pie & Custard … A fine drizzle had started when we came out so we made for the ferry from Devonport to Tor Point. There was a half hour wait before the Downderry bus, so we went into a small brown pub full of sailors & drank cider, before rattling back to camp feeling merrier than usual …

No record of that Sunday

when five of us and one mountain woman
climbed up the Pyg track from Pen-y-Pass,

Crib Goch shaved of cloud
against a brilliant spring sky,

our feet kicking grey-pink rocks – *make no mark*
she says – *take small steps up the steep.*

We tread delicately across sprawling stones
towards Bwlch Glas above Glaslyn

and nothing she tells us
do I forget.

I don't say much
but for the first time –

feet on rock –
I'm where I'm meant to be.

Where was that farmhouse
deep in the hills

where late in the day we stopped?
Fruit cake and sweet hot tea

which sustained me
across the miles   the years

Ninth April 1943, Downderry

And still this premature summer continues. The skies, a clear
blue haze, the sea their counterpart, licking lazily at the long
reefs of black rocks, the sea gulls wheeling white against the sky.
The full riot of spring has burst around us. I've never known
weather so hot in April before. The sun has streamed down all
day on the hot pink earth. The young corn is leaping up to meet
the sun, & the trees wore their hazy green spotted branches
between the ethereal blue above & the solid red beneath.

Ninth April 2020, Isle of Wight

Today relentless sun
not meant for spring

the sky's blue helmet
shuts us in

I long for April showers
and shifting cloud

instead we're locked down
by heat

the tractors mash red earth
to dust

the chine clay set
to rock

I turn my mind
to sea

take my first chill swim
my limbs are silver-cold

Tenth April 1943, Downderry

On watch, yes, on 'night bind'. A small darkened room, half
under the ground. Little bright lights glowing & flickering

machinery that whirrs & is silent, & whirrs again. Men & women, hot or calm as their type dictates, bending over instruments & watching, leaning over maps & plotting & passing plots over the tie lines to the main plotting room. Spare 'bodies' on their hour off, sitting in odd corners round the Ops room, & reading or writing. Constant cups of strong tea & thick powdery cocoa. Toast & margarine with baked beans or sausages spread on top & eaten with the aid of fingers. Bomber sweeps & the intense concentration needed to keep up with the plots & identities & added to this, the excitement of a few hostilities swooping around.

Tenth January 2020, Isle of Wight (on watch)

Here, at my desk, yes,
oblongs of pale sun
held in the lattices,
a shuffle of papers,
a red cyclamen
on the windowsill
shedding its petals,
a wooden letter holder
spilling stray papers,
the cat, tail coiled,
curled beside my laptop,
the flicker of fingers,
coffee in a white mug,
half drunk, gone cold,
three oatcakes stacked,

tractors shuddering
down the lane, windows
rattling, attention shifting.
Our times collide –
illuminated
animated
alongside.

Twelfth April 1943

Back in Cosford Hospital for radiant heat treatment on both skin grafts.

So here I am back at Cosford in Shropshire for a week ... It seems queer to be back in a large camp again, after the hothouse atmosphere & small gossip of Downderry.

This morning, while I was working in the Burns Centre, arranging photographs, who should walk in but one of the old crowd of last September, 'Big'. He is now a Flying Officer, has grown a moustache, & has developed more hair on his head. It is peculiar, that on re-meeting with someone whom one was very familiar with in the past, that two distinctly different sensations should immediately spring up. The first is that of timelessness & naturalness, as though nothing could be more usual than this chance meeting. And then immediately time counters it, & your friend takes on the colouring of past events, like a character that has just stepped out of a history book.

your words

your youthful voice
have taken on
the subtle shades
of close knowing

your thoughts floating
across the years
as if I knew you
as you were

but what if
suddenly
you were here
before me

how I know it's you
and yet
how new
how strange

Twelfth May 1943, Downderry

A day full of minor events. To begin with I had an argument
with Sergeant Chalmens over the hut inspection that Flying
Officer Williams was supposed to have carried out today. The
hut floor had to be exceptionally well polished, beds staggered,
& only one book, one box & one photo left on our shelf. It
was the one book that annoyed me, & which I queried when

the Sergeant came in. Naturally, as most sergeants appear to be impregnated with a strong flavour of Fascism, the argument became involved. Culture & democracy were upheld by the hut & rigid discipline combined with an uncritical mind were furiously hurled at us by an irate sergeant.

Not one to back down, without a fight,
once you shoved a bucket on the head
of a difficult colleague who'd sniped
at you and threatened your department.
I remember his name, but not
what came of it. I suspect that you won
in the end.

And you and me of course. We would not
back down. *Compromise*, a counsellor said
when I was young. We were passionate
in argument and neither could quite
refrain from hurling comments spiked
with memories we knew would hurt. What
stopped us in the end?

Twenty-second May 1943, Downderry

I got let in for a parade at Tor Point, in fact the whole of the WAAF on C Watch had to go, as it was our free day. After lunch when we were getting ready, it poured with rain, so we had to polish our great coat buttons as well as our tunics.

Finally 30 of us were packed like cattle into a large RAF lorry & swerved & skidded our way to Tor Point. It was Wings for Victory week, so the Air Force was in the vanguard of the parade. There is a curious emotionalism that sweeps you up on a parade. (The Nazi mind has evidently realised this only too well.) Most of us had grumbled exceedingly over having to go 'a frightful bind' – 'Women weren't made for marching' etc, but when the march began, when the band broke into our Air Force march as the salute was taken at the Cenotaph, more than one confessed afterwards over having felt lumpy about the throat.

Remembrance

Your good navy coat. Your medals pinned
to the lapels. My old walking stuff,

not smart enough I knew, although you said
The Good Lord wouldn't mind. But anger flared

between us as it always had. We stood
beside the Cenotaph outside your village church.

Lump in my throat. I saw you salute
although my eyes could not meet yours.

Names of the dead were read. We went inside
to pray. That was your last Remembrance Day.

Nineteenth June 1943, Downderry

Today I went to the small Methodist Chapel in the village. There was only myself, another WAAF & two elderly men present, & no preacher arrived. One of the men volunteered the prayers, the other read the first lesson & I the second, & together we chose & sung five hymns. This is not the first service at which I have assisted.

Sundays

you created pools of light
with garden flowers

Saturday afternoons for years
you and my father swept the aisle

you fought the rearguard
of 'elderly' resistance to change

sometimes you read the lesson
your voice unfurling to the furthest pew

despite the frowns
you bought a new lectern

where just once I stood to read –
'For Sleep or Death' –

the day your white coffin rested
alight with flowers

Twenty-fourth June 1943, Downderry

Midsummer Night, & the hills & sea around the camp are steeped in quiet mystery.

So much has happened today. The afternoon in the Ops block was busy, & we worked five hours without a break, or a respite from the head sets, which made the ears sore & tender. On coming off watch we learnt that a plane which all afternoon had been circling the towers & cliffs had crashed into a hill a mile or two away. The kite was smashed into atoms, & the pilot, a 21 year old Australian, thrown out & killed instantly. He was brought back to our sick quarters for a little while. This sounds a sad note for the ending of this book... not the ending of the whole journal – for I have another book in which to carry on. I have grown fond of the familiar blue covers, & the book has become part of the things I have loved & feared & found interesting in the past eighteen months. So now I must cease writing, & hope that the next book will show the same sympathetic understanding towards my scribbling pen.

the ink once blue,
fades to sea-grey

but the letters, alert, tilt
towards the next journal

Cento with my mother

We didn't know what to do with our hats –
long green tassels inventing their own devils

the orange gloom of over-weighted buses
clothes sprayed across the floor

the stiff and ragged straw
the blackbird calls from next door

I don't think I shall ever forget
the iron framework, the stacked biscuits

patches on the wall where photos hung
a sink full of empty tins

a green enamelled beetle
a fender & an easel

a voice on the radio grates
in the sticky air

the damp tramps in
along stone passages

a rumour that primroses have been seen
down the lane to Brownbread Street

do you remember the day
we went to Pear Tree Farm?

Bill Tingley, Peggy Bartlett, Edna & Sue
dusty roads, little bees, sweet peas & lupins

jagged masonry scratches the sky
the church house bombed to the ground

the Old Hut sleeps alone
I want to go home

a woodlouse hurries to shelter under a stone
evening sun trickles between blast walls

a brown creosoted smell from the fence
a man loosening the earth his foot on a fork

a thin wind weakening
cringing yellow leaves

catastrophes shrivel
to a skin of a worm in the sun

how will the end come?

rhythmic phrases   regular cadences

Mary Winkle & Maud Alexander

air threaded with resin

a sputter of stars

Your second book

scratched and shined by age –

smudged with black ink –
binding frayed in strips and threads

but your name still retains
its cursive flaunt

price 1/8d stamped
inside the front page

your handwriting whirls
blue loops vanishing to mauve

pages shot through
with loose poems

notes, dates, addresses
quotes, times, places –

to meet Nissan Hut Three
tags – *ut me miseratum* –

now everything's loosening

it won't stand

much more handling

One more night bind is nearly over & the watch with weary sleepy faces, cleans up the block ready for the relieving watch. The first thing we shall say to the new watch will be 'What's for breakfast?' Then, carrying our blankets with the girls wearing their slacks, we shall straggle back down the village street to the 'B' site & bed. How lovely it will be to be back again in 'civvy street' & able to spend every night asleep in bed. In years to come, we shall probably all look back with some sort of affection upon these wearisome night watches, & little will remain in our memories but the comradeship of these nights. Those self cooked suppers out in the Rest Hut about midnight, & the table strewn with baked beans, toast & pint mugs of steaming cocoa, & the whole ringed round with jovial, shouting advice about cooking, grinning faces. Perhaps there will be 'bags of activity' in the Ops Room & everyone will be excited & a little strained & the whole atmosphere will be taut-tensioned. Maybe nothing much will be happening & there will be chatter & laughter & sudden silences, & a few odd sleepy bodies curling up in blankets on the floor for an hour or two's disturbed slumber. However, at last it's all over for another four days & we can stumble back to our beds until the afternoon.

Bind

How did you look back on those night binds –
comradeship, cocoa, cups of tea? If I'd read
your diary before you died, would I have asked

does your past still bind you? Or was it something more than
that – a kind of flow between your selves – young and old –
like one of your rich silk threads lighting white cotton?

Did your diaries, days contained between
familiar covers, bound with frayed blue tape,
illuminate old age when your present blurred?

Am I bound to you, your past? Or will it end
once I shut your books? For now
your paragraphs are lanterns. I peer into the Ops Room

then watch you straggle back to B site
as if all it takes is faded ink to bind the particles
of me and you until *at last it's all over*

and we stumble back to our beds

Thirtieth July 1943, Downderry

All day long the earth has been drenched with sun, & the little
village street running parallel to the shore has been vivid with
strong colour. Black shadow & white wall gleaming over the
road, scarlet rose & green doors & beyond it all, modulated by
so many shades of blue, that unconquerable creature, the sea.

My last sea view of you

three months before you died –
the wide sweep of a beach,
low tide, a far out sea,
us all scattered on shining sand
when suddenly you stopped,
unlaced your shoes,
unpeeled your tights.
Through pools of gold,
saltwater-lapped,
your wobbling run began
across the ripple marks
towards the waves,
years and pain
dissolved, an arc
of blue above,
the sea, the sea
within, within, within

Birthday Album

Ninth August 1943, Downderry

My 23rd birthday. It is one of those gloriously still & golden
August mornings, with the trees & the grass ablaze with dew.
A morning that makes Time a matter of indifference & Youth
eternal … And my kid brother, nearly grown up. One never
seems to notice people altering or growing until they have
definitely changed. Alan in the present is always Alan, yet the

past & present yet to come are so welded with the present that they become one person. It is as though a single thread of distinctive and unique colouring was woven together from the beginning of Time, straight through a multitudinous pattern of colour into Eternity.

Ninth August 1930

On your 10th birthday,
here's a photograph
beside your brother,
one neat, full plait brushed
over your shoulder,
combed fringe, flowered frock,
filmy gauze, lips curved,
smile already yours.

Ninth August 1944, Bawdsey

My 24th birthday, clear & hot, with the brown gold corn fast being cut & stacked. I have been home, but had to leave early to be back in time for night watch.

Ninth August 1990

Your 70th birthday,
elbows on a gold stook

we gaze, off camera
in the same direction,

eyes narrowed against
the sun. We smile, my lips

closed, yours parted, the dip
and fold of flesh which meets

the corners of our mouths,
the swell of cheek, the play

of lines in sync, despite
the gap of years; your hair

silver-fair, sun-hat perched
on your curls, mine sun-streaked.

Our noses jut and shine
in fierce harmony.

My blue vest reveals
sunburnt skin, your neck yoked

with cream lace. The shadow
of a stalk bracelets both

our forearms, the same veins
sign the backs of our hands.

Ninth August 1945, Pevensey

My 25th birthday, but even after a quarter of a century of life, I do not seem to have gone far. I am singularly unsuccessful either in a career or marriage. In mental age, no older than 18 or 19 years, but the added six years of experience has undoubtedly given a little depth to shallow waters.

Ninth August 2020

Do you have to be alive
to celebrate? Here we are
today, your centenary.
No photo of course, but I
see you, your hair white at last,
the brown-gold corn being cut
in the field behind your house,
your smile welcoming me home.

Twelfth August 1943 (on leave)

No matter how desperately you cling to every moment of leave, still will Time defeat you.

Twelfth April 2020

Down at Atherfield Bay, I'm on long leave, distant cliffs dissolving in streams of early mist. The time is place-time, not human time, leaving me no trace of when I came or left.

An evening of gardening & renewing acquaintance of every path, every tree, every plant

Three weeks of lockdown, social distancing, slowing down

& the leaping delight over a new blossom that was not there on the last leave.

& a new courgette plant, not there yesterday, nudging out of the compost.

The row of friendly books in the bedroom, each one begging to be opened & read this time.

Long unopened books release the steadiness this time demands: *The Prelude*; *The Country Child*; *A Traveller in Time*; *The Body in the Library*; *The Seafarer* …

Friends to be seen, shopping to be done & a thousand & one things to be talked about.

Friends to be waved at, shopping forgotten, silences opening…

All these have to be crushed into a few short days –

The days stretch. Perhaps we shall learn to lull in hours which swing and dip like hammocks.

Surely this generation will have learnt the art of *précis*,

Will this generation learn the art of being still?

of how to cut out the non essential

> Of how to sow seeds – radish, rocket, kale, to forage for wild
> garlic, dandelion, fat hen

If we are wise – will we be wise?

> perhaps we shall learn to discriminate between the real &
> the unreal

at the top of the chine a kestrel skims past me, fence height, less
than a metre away

> to decide on the things of greatest worth upon which action
> must be taken immediately

Twenty-fourth September 1943, Downderry

The Ops Room is cold & comparatively silent, for we are all
rather weary & heavy eyed. We should like to 'get down' on the
floor in a blanket, but the supervisor is still here. There is no
activity. My mind wanders over & round silly things & in my
sleepy state it is easy to attach importance to small happenings.
The hum of the air filtration plant seems gigantic & ominous,
like some huge vampire poised over the block. The set clicks &
whirs intermittently & odd disjointed conversations begin suddenly & end even more abruptly. My eyes are sore & heavy with
watching. I would give nearly all I have for a good bed. How
slowly the clock moves, how unending the stretch of seconds the

large finger ticks away. In another hour & a half it will be my turn to take over the observing. How shall I ever keep awake?

Fifteenth January 2020, HMP

In the guts of HMP, where I run my prison writers' workshops: an absence of windows; a muffled gloom from the skylight; a fluorescent glare; fetid air; sore eyes; the clang of gates, the blare of radios; an air-conditioning unit broken, hovering above us like a giant hawk; intense bursts of concentration; swish of hands across the page; click of pens, words like sparks lighting the stuffiness; gulps of water; glints of humour; the need to stand and stretch; bands of headache gripping the skull; shared incarceration; swipes of imagination; flights of memory;

kindness, griefs, joys.

Twenty-seventh October 1943, Great Bromley

I sit by the fire in the reading room & try to write, & people talk & I find myself drawn into their conversations. First it is a discussion on the Germans & post war plans for Germany – are there any? – the flatness of the average modern woman's figure – midwifery & having babies – London shows & Augustus John … … and so on & on, & I mix myself up in ideas, become entangled in other people's personalities & at last cry out against this slavery of myself. I think how good it would be to sit down disinterestedly outside another character without feeling the tug towards the vortex of each new being. To be free enough from the toils of ordinary life, to stand back from the whole & pause & know reality ...

Portrait of the artist

Did you at last cut free from the confines
of others – bonds of *mother, wife*?
To burst out in fiery lines –
artist, beyond the toils of daily life?

Look, there. Unbound from *mother, wife*
you set your easel in the kitchen,
artist twisting coils of daily life,
painting saucepan, kettle, wooden spoon.

You set your easel in the kitchen,
you lay out your acrylics on the shelf.
You paint saucepan, kettle, wooden spoon,
a fiery head. You look back at yourself.

You pick acrylics from the shelf.
You block out specks that grit your vision.
Your fiery head looks back. At you, yourself?
You cleave yourself. Artistic fusion.

Block out the specks that grit your vision.
Burst out in fiery lines.
Cleave yourself. Artistic fusion.
Within the confines, freedom.

Eighteenth December 1943, Great Bromley (12 midnight)

Christmas draws nearer, the skies grow greyer, the long evenings are more intensely dark & the crowds of shoppers denser & more panic stricken. It is cold on watch. There are five of us on this the first half of the night – Stan, Len, Bert, Tom and myself, with the Supervisor in her office. Nothing happens, everybody is sleepy & dull witted. Two people are nattering eternally over the 'line' & I have to sit and listen. It is time for another cup of tea & perhaps some toast.

Winter twilight, Isle of Wight

It is four o'clock. The sky darkens, restless grey.
Nearing the shortest day. I push back sleep,
tracing the fine black outline
of the chestnut tree, where patches
of grey silk sky stretch between branches.
A cloud lifts like a blind. A slit of light above the hill.
A pale sunset. The tree turns brilliant black.
It is time to go out and dig leeks for soup.

Twenty-seventh January 1944, Great Bromley

For the last three or four weeks I have been struggling against an ever-growing depression, a sense of defeat & inadequacy. There have been short periods when for a little while I have risen above it, but I have always sunk again.

Voices

Cold fingers point scorn into the little recesses of my mind
Enclosed in a dark cell & sunk to the centre of the earth
I hammer on the walls in indignation at my imprisonment
yet cling to the dark solidity of my obscurity
no way out of the net of self criticism
out of touch, out of rhythm – how
can I re-kindle my zeal for life –
utter desolation, nothing left
but a heap of
well picked
bones

last night   last night   last night –

I
began to
read *De Profundis*
again. Now – I read
& understand clinging to
every phrase – however bewildering,
heart-rending my experiences I cannot help
revelling in them. White & black the twilight
dulled to merging points by spits of blown rain,
trees scrape the sky in twisted torture & no sun
goes down in the west – What shall I make this into?
Something with paint and line? Rhythmical phrases?
The rain has slashed the roofs of the huts all afternoon.
Wet leaves slime the concrete.

Today – I saw the first snowdrop.
The dead wood, the tangled stalks of winter to be cut away

– the thought of spring

Twelfth February 1944, Great Bromley

I have spent my last 36 hours with Lynette … It has all gone so quickly, & yet it seems so long since it started … We sat in front of the living room fire at her parents, eating supper & talking, talking. Even in bed, we talked till we fell asleep, our lips still murmuring… It has all gone so quickly & yet it seems so long since it started … the soft gloomy blue of a London evening, the dusky sea of Trafalgar Square & the cool sweetness of the moon over Tunbridge Wells. We paused for a moment, Lynette & I, on the hill overlooking a little valley, with the town beyond. We have stood together like that so often in the past, as children, at the close of day at the end of all play & work, just standing silently, side by side, looking & listening.

The Call

When she died
I picked up,
tracked you down
in *Les Landes*.

She was ill,
you said, *and*
I was not
there, no one

at her side
at close of
day, end of
work and play.

Your grief was
dusk, night fall
seas of loss,
but now I

think she is
with you, no
words, but still,
side by side.

In memory of Lynette Garrard, 1920 – 1977

Fourteenth February 1944, Great Bromley

A day clear & cold, the brown pink earth alive, thinly sweet with the force of new life driving upwards from the dead darkness below. The fat budded trees are pregnant with spring & leaping laughter is caught in every living plant shaken by the wind. Watches churn thro' the days with heavy monotony. We wait.

The Second Front is expected this spring. Last night the raid over this area was snappy, the barrage heavy & phosphorous & incendiary bombs were dropped. The light went out, & we spent a little while in the dust under our beds. I have a heavy cold. I am preparing the second month's work for my correspondence course in child psychology, & getting ready to paint the black-out in the Rest Hut – bright, flamboyant legends & ballet scenes – Le Spectre de la Rose, Giselle, Faust & perhaps The Ancient Mariner …

Painting on a loose leaf of paper, circa 1998

No words stumble across your page. Your sketch
propped on my desk, tugs me in, sparking
thoughts which flicker till I'm stranded on this
island of looking, which is art, which is you,
the artist seeing. Who is that figure
staring out to sea on the jagged cliff edge
beneath a pale wash of sky? Below, a gorge
sheers away, a rush of rock, a dash of blue.

My fingers touch-type as your eye fixes me
in its vision. You breathe this landscape
where I'm at home. Your marks – of ink,
crayon, paint, your smudges, jiggles, daubs, lines,
engage my senses till I give myself the slip,
reeled in to grit and grain and salt and hiss.

Seventeenth May 1944, Great Bromley.

Could they have called it any other month but May? The May trees are thick clotted with white & pink blossom, the branches hardly able to stir with the wind. Petal upon white petal mass against the blue sky. Most of all, the may around here is white, a startling sudden white, so that it amazes you when you come upon a glistening hedge banked up before a clear sky. There is something exhilarating & quickening in the sight, almost a slight catch of fear at all that whiteness. Summer is here, the grasses are tall & feathery, the lupins are out in their pale spires of colour & every cottage garden mocks at war & disillusionment & flings its laughing abundance of colour, sweet perfumes & little humming bees into the face of pain & falsehood…. Restrictions are still closing in, & there is now a limited radius in which we can travel. Everyone waits, everything is still. The days are long, calm & hot, halcyon days to be remembered as forerunners of a Great Storm or a Quiet Miracle. Yesterday we had a pep talk by the Group captain – we are growing tired of pep talks & continual exhortations to hold on for the 'Big Push' …

Towards D Day

(Prose sculpture, created from diary entries
leading up to D Day.)

           & here   now

engines churning   & rooks unsettled caw & flutter

sweep returning	& gnats dance
crouched windows	& a meeting of bean-fields perfumes time
air queued up	& green singing
paths tired & difficult	& a startling glistening hedge quickening today
concrete focus	& clotted branches a sudden startling white
passes stopped	& pools of sunlight streak through regulations
restrictions close in	& shirts & stockings hung out to air
limited grumble	& little humming bees
dull black of Camp	& a catch of whiteness
Ops room stuffy	& call it pink stir
war & disillusionment	& pale lupin spires fling falsehood
the Great Storm	& a Quiet Miracle

& here   now

Sixth June 1944, Great Bromley

The waiting is over. The quiet is broken.

Early this morning Allied Troops, paratroops & navy landed in Normandy & the north coast of France. Over the radio, a constant stream of alerts & warnings are being broadcast in all languages of the northwest European countries. I woke in the night or rather early this morning, to hear a ceaseless roar of aircraft going over & wondered then if the invasion could be starting.

Twenty-first June 1944, Midsummer Day, Great Bromley

I am sitting on the grass at the side of the crossroads at Little Bromley. The warm red brick, red tiled vicarage is behind me, surrounded by little sunny lawns & shaded by the lovely foliage of English trees. All would be silent but for the endless roar of aircraft bent on war. The cuckoo sings late this year. The hay is cut, laid out to dry & stacked. The long summer grasses in the hedgerows fall beneath the sharp scythe of an old countryman. The cottage gardens, abound in roses & Canterbury bells, the hedges glow with the wild pink rose & are sweet with the scent of honeysuckle. Summer! England! And I in these am alive.

Photographs

as if by now with artist's eye
you'd learnt to frame yourself
to flirt with the camera –

three WAAFs on the beach
and it's you whose cleavage shows,
whose poise is perfect, long legs
elegantly crossed, whose gaze glows,

while I still stiffen, lacking your ease,
your way of saying
Look at me

but once you're over eighty
something shifts – see here you are
dressed in Air Force Blue
to give a talk about the war

tie knotted, shoes shined,
shoulders skewed by loss
and in your true blue eyes

what I'd missed before –

humility

Second August 1944, Bawdsey

The heavy green of the trees is covered with a little grey dust; &
the wasp disturbs the warm air with a yellow stinging hum. I
am disappointed for I have not moved to Sussex but to Suffolk,
near Felixstowe. I arrived yesterday with Bill, Peggy, Edna & Sue
& went down to Hythe on the same day. So I have left Bromley

behind after 9 months & I feel a little Bromley-sick. The block is stuffier, fuller & busier & the discipline side is tighter & stickier. I want to go home.

I want to go home

all your youth you knew
what it was to flit
but each manse became the solace
you'd call home

when I left home
for northern days of mist and rain,
you never said, but understood
how much I longed to go home

if I have to leave
my loved patch of earth
when all around is flailed and slashed
will I still want to go home?

in your last house
I said *time to move?*
you said, heart-torn,
I don't want to leave

an airless ward –
a very nice hotel
but now I'd like
to go home

the hospice bed
a white cocoon
you seemed serene
as if you knew

it was time to go home

Seventeenth September 1944, St Rhadagunds, Isle of Wight

I've been posted on the Isle of Wight. I'm very lucky in this posting but I don't feel it will be for long… and it certainly has not been for long. On 19th September at 18.00 hours, the station went 'off the air' & finally closed down. Meanwhile the place has been turned into a holiday camp & except for a few minor fatigues, we are out in the sun all day & dancing all night. In & out of the sunny room which is our bedroom, the butterflies drift, thinking that summer is eternal & a sharp frost nothing but a jealous streak of my imagination. There are comfortable noises about the house & garden, people pottering around with odd jobs as though they had all day, which indeed they have. There is peace & colour, warmth & gaiety & room for the mind & heart to expand.

St Rhadagunds

We never visited St Rhadagunds together,
although I lived so close. You never had the chance
to say, *Let's go*. We did not take the footpath to the sea,
past bunkers now grassed over, or point out

the concrete bases where the radar masts had stood.
No bee orchids were seen along the cliffs.

We did not walk up the drive arm in arm,
nor idle in the sun. No butterflies drifted
through open windows, as if winter would never come.
We did not try to work out which room you slept in.
Your eyes did not light up. That was not your laughter.
You did not recall the dancing. We did not have that day.

First November 1944, Pevensey

The War goes on & it is not expected to end before spring or
early summer. We are stuck in Holland, the Germans are flooding
the land & the winter sets in.

00.00 hours. And so, on night watch again. The strong moon-
light is breaking the countryside up into violent patchwork.
Everything has reached the fantastic, nothing is quite real. The
transport rushed quickly thro' the clear, cold air & we sat
hunched closely together for warmth. The disjointed conversation was spotted with 'Ops' talk.

'They had 900 last night.'
'Well, I hope we don't tonight.'
'I could go to sleep right now.'
Then, 'Did you hear those kites roaring over about seven?'
'Probably Berlin, like the ones this morning.'
'Or Cologne.'
'Not much left to bomb in Cologne, they say it's only a heap.'

Silence for a while, then a sudden burst of song, & a cottage window curtained red, glows in passing, the churchyard lying naked in silver light. Again, a cigarette hurtles from the transport & spatters onto the hard road & small talk limps into being once more.

Kites

I'd always thought
the way you spoke

of kites was show off –
a kind of flaunting of 'your' war.

I made a point
of never asking exactly what you meant,

just as you made a point
of relishing the word.

On your last flight,
five months before your death,

you said as we took off,
soaring above Jersey airport,

*I just love being in a kite
don't you?*

Flight
there's nothing like it,

and I suppressed
a wince of spite,

but now, at last, I check
kite   RAF slang   aircraft

and catch an echo
of your delight.

Seventh December 1944, Pevensey

… the stove nearly red hot, twigs for tomorrow's lighting resiny before the fire. It is quiet too. This is a dull little camp but somehow I don't feel so restless or discordant as before. Anyway I wouldn't miss being alive for the possession of the whole Universe. And now, I'm going to have a bath – how I love a bath …

You always loved a bath

the benison of water, almost scalding hot,
the steam and scent of soap, the sea-slip-slap,
the lick, the lap, the limbs unlock,
the merry, frothing splash of taps,
the antidote to gloom and grief,
such great good humour I could hug the world,
the sense of safe within the water's keep.

You called me once when you were in the bath,
and, though beaming still, you said
It's horrid being old. No thought
then of age's creep through my strong body,
but somehow I knew what you meant –
the lines you fought so hard to hide,
the loosening skin, the veins,
that slight uncertainty of step.

Twenty-fourth January 1945, Pevensey

Snow – soft & white, covering & rolling over everything. White hills curl & melt into the skyline. The trees, no longer black and snaky, but one fairie creature sparkling in gracious loveliness. But the greatest miracle of all is the barbed wire. The snow has disguised it as the most beautiful white creeper with delicate tendrils curving up & dipping over, a flashing whirling growth of feathery fronds, rhythmed into a long twisting hedge.

When I cross the prison yard
in certain kinds of light

I marvel
at the shadow

of razor wire
which flourishes

fantastic loops
across the concrete –

and look – there
a blackbird perched

on the highest spiral,
inscribing the sky with song.

Eighteenth February 1945, Pevensey

It is more beautiful than they ever meant it to be, holding the
moon & black branches in its dark water depths, still against the
stone lips, holding it from the huts it centres. Rectagonal static
water pool, built to put out the enemy fire bombs & surrounded
by our little huts. Another world that wasn't dreamed of by the
hands that built it, descendant of a Roman courtyard, this slip
of water surrounded by walls & courts, domed in with sky.

Anti-aircraft site, Isle of Wight

Set in a concrete slab
slipped over the cliffs

now half sunk in sand
for waves to sweep and shape

a rusted metal ring,
red, ochre, gold

holding the sky
inside a round eye of sea

a sudden vision
of another world

Eighth May 1945, Pevensey

VE day & peace in Europe. A very warm day, almost inclined
to be thundery. A general air of festivity drapes the camp. Flags
& decorations are being put up in the canteen for the dance
tonight & most of the girls are busy in the Cookhouse preparing
trifles & jellies… I don't know why but somehow I don't feel
very festive. I think I would rather spend the whole day with one
or two friends, out in the country… Later I went to the
Thanksgiving service in the little congregational church at
Herstmonceux. It was packed with people & did they sing! And
now there is the hurly burly of the dance & the gay colours of
the frocks we are going to wear.

Eleventh May 1945, Pevensey

The blackout is over & the light once more leaps into the night.

Cento with my mother

I saw a black snake in the woods today
    slipping through the crackle of dead leaves

the sad cakes in the funny little café
    the strange similarity of crowded faces

a scrap of blue sky
    above the blast walls and sand bags

small winds twist through vacant arches
    of door-less gaps

dirty cups on the plotting table
    my skin tingles with nettle rash

patches of tiredness
    punctuated by leaps into life

I lie on a lower bunk in the barrack room
    watching little lights lunge up into the dark

spattered sparks of a cigarette
    flung from the transport

– the incorrigible Mary Hazlitt has gone, Louise
    the dynamic Canadian with the just too yellow hair –

low mists linger in the meadows at dusk
    tiny snails slink

no oasis but in myself
    nothing but a sandy hollow

you have to fight
    to keep your inner self alive

      a tall mystery of purple foxgloves

      a green kindness of weeds

      for the rest of my life –

Sixteenth August 1945, Pevensey

We are in a world that has peace. That is, if peace means simply no bloodshed. At midnight on August 14th the Allies gave the news of the surrender of the Japanese. Everyone immediately got up & plunged through the darkness across to the Canteen. We held a riotous dance until about 4 o'clock, beer flowed freely, the pianist hammered heatedly & all whirled in delighted pandemonium. Last night – the first of the two VJ days – we spent on the village green at Herstmonceux. There was a huge bonfire & a royal pyramid of English oak logs with the rich flames climbing until they flickered into sparks & thinning away to smoke, passed up to the stars.

The end of my leave

and the end of my book

I turn back to the first page,
cream paper, brown-flecked with age.

A finger print.
Yours? Or mine?

And then
your name

Evelyn M. Wilkinson

Notes

Wherever possible I have preserved the authenticity of the diaries, including any idiosyncrasies of spelling or punctuation.

'Ampersand'

A Black Mariah – A police van used to transport prisoners.

'On the couch'

While in the WAAF, my mother had to have some of the veins on her left leg, removed because they were sore and easily bruised. She was operated on by Sir Archibald Hector McIndoe CBE FRCS (4th May 1900 – 11th April 1960), a pioneering plastic surgeon from New Zealand who worked for the Royal Air Force during the Second World War. This was followed by skin grafts from her thigh and salt baths to help healing. They weren't varicose veins and it's not clear what caused this proliferation of lumpy, uncomfortable veins. My sister and I called her scarred leg her 'bad leg'. We have both inherited a few tiny ones.

'Once a place has hold of you'

Lepe – a beach west of Southampton, which looks across to the Isle of Wight. It was a favourite drive for my parents, who would have a stroll and a cup of tea looking out towards the Island.

'Christmas 1942'

NAAFI – Navy, Army and Air Force Units.

'Limerstone Down'

'Here and there, like green glass bubbles, old barrows…' – The barrows referred to are probably Bronze Age barrows found in this area. The closest to Yatesbury (Wiltshire) is the Old Bath Road Tumulus, now part of the Wessex Ridgeway. It was damaged in World War 2 in order to insert an anti-aircraft post.

'No record of that Sunday'

The Sound is a deep inlet in the English Channel near Plymouth. Hoe is derived from the Old English 'Hoe', meaning high ground. The reference is to Sir Francis Drake who was said to be playing bowls on Plymouth Hoe when the Spanish Armada was sighted in the English Channel.

'Ninth April 2020, Isle of Wight'

Chine – The word 'chine' derives from the Anglo Saxon 'chinan' meaning a gap or a yawn. On the Isle of Wight (and also in parts of Hampshire and Dorset) a number of small rivers flow down from high points and abruptly meet the coast. Chines are formed by the erosion of soft clays and sands caused by the waters flowing out to sea. The poet Mimi Khalvati who went to school on the Island, memorably described a chine as 'a form of urgency to reach the sea.' (*The Chine*, 2002)

'On Watch'

Tie lines – telecommunication circuits between two telephone exchanges.

'Sundays'
For Sleep or Death – A poem by Ruth Pitter (1897 – 1992).

'Cento with my mother'
Cento – a poem made up entirely of lines from other poets' writing. It sometimes, though not always, has 100 lines. Cento is also Italian for a patchwork garment.

Mary Winkle & Maud Alexander – Mary and Maud were probably two fellow WAAFs on the same posting and perhaps in the same hut as my mother.

'Your Second Book'
Ut me miseratum translates as: Take pity on me.

'Bind'
Bind – RAF slang: a tedious job; to bind – to tie or hold together.

'Birthday Album'
Stook – A number of sheaves of grain, stacked upright to dry together.

'Fifteenth January 2020, HMP'
The Ops Room was the radar operations room, where the plotters, using a long stick, worked with the sightings received from the Observer Corps or Radar Scans to trace the position of RAF fighter squadrons and the enemy across the sector maps of the south coast, so that senior officers could direct the battle.

Description of Ops room, from a later piece by Evelyn M. Wilkinson titled 'On Radar Watch around and after D Day':

> The huge computer-like set around the radar screen, with plotting table behind it, was more than ever the focus of tense and excited attention that day of all days. In the darkness of the Ops Room, people were drugged by the brilliance of the signals beating their way across the screen, & the china-graf pencils poised over the gleaming plotting table began to weave a web-like pattern over the enemy coastline and sea.

'Voices'

Collaged using diary extracts between 27th January 1944 and late 1945.

'I want to go home'

As the daughter of a Methodist minister my mother was used to moving to a new manse every three years.

'Anti-aircraft site, Isle of Wight.'

The remains of anti aircraft sites can still be found on the Isle of Wight. On the beach at Grange Chine, on the south coast of the Island, one slipped from the cliff top because of coastal erosion.

Acknowledgements

Acknowledgements are due to the editors of *Scintilla, The Journal of the Vaughan Association* and to *Orbis* magazine, in which several of these poems appeared. Also to The Understory Conversation where the poem 'St Rhadagunds' is discussed with poet Lorna Dowell (theunderstoryconversation.com).

I would like to thank poets Lorna Dowell and Robyn Bolam for their support, invaluable response and editing suggestions throughout the development of *Ampersand*.

Thanks also to the Spring Poets' Poetry Workshops in Havant and to the Solent Poets Workshops for their steady encouragement, feedback and support.